T0154994

FENCE LINE

Curtis Bauer's poems are as abundant in feeling and imaginative energy as the soil of his native Midwest is abundant in natural life. The Poems in *Fence Line* are impressive in their grace and precision and verbal strength and integrity. But they are astonishing in their beauty, luminousness, and human accuracy.

—Vijay Seshadri

In meditations on his adopted country, Spain, and in praise songs to the American Midwest, Bauer conjures the lives of those who work the land. When "the dead return as/ the sound of blowing crickets," they do so in a place of stark windbreaks and feedlots. "We all need a good branding now and then," the wry speaker declares in "Waiting," one of several poems that explore rural boyhood and the construction of masculinity. Tenderness informs Bauer's sharp observations: of the beloved, one speaker offers these musical lines: "she wants to be a bird/ flying above Barcelona." These poems vivify the landscapes that remain with the one who leaves—and returns, changed.

—Robin Becker

FENCE LINE

Curtis Bauer

Winner of the John Ciardi Prize for Poetry
selected by Christopher Buckley

BkMk Press
University of Missouri-Kansas City

BkMk Press
University of Missouri-Kansas City
5101 Rockhill Road
Kansas City, Missouri 64110
(816) 235-2558 (voice)
(816) 235-2611 (fax)
bkmk@umkc.edu
http://www.umkc.edu/bkmk

Cover art: Landscape, copyright© Robert Bauer.
Courtesy of Forum Gallery, private collection, New York.
Book Design: Susan L. Schurman
Managing Editor: Ben Furnish
Associate Editor: Michelle Boisseau

Thanks to:
Bill Beeson, Susan Cobin, Ryan Cunningham, Greg Field,
Steve Gehrke, Jesi Hylan, Jeannie Irons, Elaine K. Lally, Philip Miller, Eugene Murphy, Michael Nelson, Nick Serafin, William Trowbridge,
Maryfrances Wagner

Library of Congress Cataloging-in-Publication Data

Bauer, Curtis, 1970-
    Fence Line / by Curtis Bauer—1st ed.
        p.cm.
    ISBN 1-886157-48-0   (pbk. : alk. paper)   1. Young men—Poetry.
    2. Spain—Poetry   3. Iowa—Poetry   I. Title.

PS3602.A935F46 2004
811'.6—dc22   2004015357

This book is set in Papyrus and Goudy Old Style type.

in memory of my grandfather

—

for Idoia

Acknowledgments

The author would like to express his grateful acknowledgment to the following publications in which some of the poems in this collection first appeared, some in earlier versions:

7 Carmine: "The Cats of Fuchosa," "After The Procession Of The Virgin Of Solitude"
Barrow Street: "Urban Landscape"
The Cortland Review: "In High Demand"
The GW Review: "A Reason For Concern," "El Paseo De Los Amantes,"
The Iconoclast: "Looking Toward Minnesota"
Illuminations: "Afterlife"
Inkwell: "On Elm Street"
The Kit-Cat Review: "Waiting"
The Larcom Review: "Thorn Tree"
Mantis: "Inside"
The Midwest Quarterly: "Rush Hour in the City of Q"
The North American Review: "Summer Storm," "Landscape with Leaves"
Parting Gifts: "During a Lull in the Conversation," "The Sound of Habitation," "The Guest," "Sketch"
Pinyon: "A Sound Like Footsteps Beside The Ocean"
Rattapallax: "Blue"
Runes: "Landscape With Swallows"*
Torre De Papel: "Landscape: Galicia With Two Figures"
The Underwood Review: "Portrait Of An Evening"
The Wallace Stevens Journal: "Eight Variations On A Landscape With Swallows"

I'd like to thank: Ben Furnish, Michelle Boisseau, and Susan Schurman for their guidance, patience and assistance in editing this book; Angela Plagmann for her creative expertise; the writing community at Sarah Lawrence College, in particular, my friends and family—Elaine Sexton, Patrick Rosal, Jeet Thayil, and Jon Wei—for their unwavering support, confidence and friendship; and I extend my profound gratitude to Christopher Buckley.

Runes published the first section of the poem "Landscape with Swallows"

In the hard, real work of life, there is meaning to be unlocked if you have the specific powers of observation and keen attention of Curtis Bauer. In a direct language, in imagery which always rises from an experiential base, in the accurate detail of a landscape, in the spare light of the past, Bauer demonstrates the considerable skill and humility necessary to uncover what epiphanies are available in a life and make some sense of the rush of experience.

Bauer knows we will not stop the problems in the world, but his is a poetry of genuine hope, of fully earned emotion. His voice is open and vulnerable to his chosen subjects, a voice that is never elevated—no sensationalism, no surface flash for its own sake here. Rather, these are poems that chip steadily away at the obdurate outcomes of fate with a realistic and mature vision, and they are deeper and more resonant for that. Bauer is faithful to the small recoveries patience and an honest approach and appreciation in poetry can yield. These are memorable poems you can believe.

—Christopher Buckley
John Ciardi Poetry Prize Judge

FENCE LINE

Contents

Acknowledgments

‍—

‍—

III

IIII

A Fence Line Running Through It

for William Schwarting

The machine shed is damp,
the dirt floor milled to powder
from years of boot and tractor
and machine traffic.
I look for the spade
I used when I was young,
when my grandfather
said dig and
I dug holes the depth
I'd been taught
so the posts would stand,
hold the miles of barbed and hog
wire dividing our ground
from Burgys, Possehls,
Stanersons and Folkmans,
dividing their cattle, their
land from ours.

Dig, he would say, and all morning,
afternoon, until it rained,
until dark, until I couldn't
lift the spade and grub
and he said enough,
I dug through dry brown
until it turned yellow clay or
black earth caked to the tip
of the steel. He taught me to measure
strength by depth, narrow the hole
around the oiled post, and
sturdy the line he'd laid
before I was old enough
to blister from work,
acquire the knowledge of straight,

of strength, cool soil, rusted
staples and splintered wood,
the knowledge of bending
spikes new, splicing wire,
swinging a hammer down hard,
the ache from hours of digging,
calloused hands and sunburn.
He trained me to rake,
tamp, stomp, pack dirt and clay,
the weight of the earth around the post,
its strength into the line.

Now the hammers, pliers and cutters
are gone. No rolls of wire
hang from the beams. No boxes
of staples and spikes jam the shelves.
The tamping stick is broken. Someone
has wrapped duct tape around the spade handle;
the steel has rusted brown and rough; a crack
climbs from the tip to the mud-caked neck.

He would say it is useless,
that things are not
like they were, and I
could repeat his words
but I have left the machine shed;
my hands have lost their calloused ridges;
my sweat, strain and ache are buried, and I
wander up and down this gravel road
dissecting Hilton Township.
I try to avoid the snow flakes and wind.

I want to touch the hands
my grandfather couldn't describe,
the hands that woke him on a plane above
Florida where he dozed
with his hand on my wife's
knee, hers on his arm.

Outside, there was endless blue—
deep and wary like his eyes—
and I knew I could not know
what he thought
when he realized the wife beside him,
the curve of her knee
was not his beside him on a wagon
filled with ear corn
they'd picked by hand, but mine,
in a plane at 30,000 feet going home.

He said he'd been dreaming,
his brother woke him
to say their steers were in the Newkirk corn.
It seemed dark and cold for summer.
And the hands, he said, were no longer his brother's;
they touched his cheek, pulled back the blankets and gripped
his fingers. After that, he couldn't tell
if he ached from grasping his spade, from picking
ear corn, or aging sixty more years and outliving his wife.

He tried to explain while we cruised above farms
and cities that the touch felt like a woman's
when she falls asleep holding your thumb.
It was smooth and trembled like grain
trickling from a bin, he said.
It felt like cold wind on a hot day.

Looking Toward Minnesota

Each night
shutting the hog-confinement doors
I'd look north toward Minnesota
wishing I could see the girl I thought I loved
to tell her how the stars looked
further south.
I'll leave out my fear
of the dark, of the possibilities
hidden in the shadows
every night before bed when
I had this final chore
to attend. I composed letters to her
as I lingered in the dark
cast by the corn crib and barn;
crickets silenced by my approach,
began their sift of clicks and chirps
as I stood still looking north.

Then there was a night
(it might have been the stench
floating up from the lagoon
or a breeze coming through the wind break,
or a distant dog's bark)
I decided to leave behind responsibility,
forget my chores,
and never see her again,
though I knew she loved
and waited for me.

There has never been a moment
equal to that when the air
in July was cool, the dew numbing my feet
and my decisions
the only ones

as the endless
cornfields murmured
Go away. Go away. Go away.

Summer Storm

I watch it approach all afternoon.
No buildings or mountains
to block the anvil-topped

thunderheads, first salt white, then
their gray-blue bottoms visible. And
now a morning-like haze edges down

the corn rows, soybean fields, the gravel
roads until the storm's not quite upon me,
but I can see it like a frontier, and I think

of the years I struggled to evade
the deluge coming down behind me
as I ran from the cattle barn to the corn crib

to the house, how I was riled by wet,
by cold and work and relieved
when the weather kept us inside. Now

standing here drenched, my hair
funneling drips around my ears and eyes,
I take my time. I walk home.

At 10 P.M.

This morning, down the street
when the geese flew over
there was a tree blazing
amber on top against a wet
gray-turning-blue sky,
crows hopped from a trash bag
to a dead rabbit, a black
squirrel sidled from the stone
wall to an elm trunk. The house
on the corner of Weslyns and Birch
looked like one dark and asleep years ago
beside a gravel road in Iowa,
the flood-light beside it pulling
lines from the barn, grain bins,
drowsy cattle in the feedlot
into the black half of yard to form
an equation I understood.

That night from behind the pine tops,
a jet cruised with its red lights flaring
on and off while I imagined
a reader looking down,
seeing the single light
glare in the sea of dark below,
a break between what she had
left and what waited. Then

she was gone, passed
through the window frame,
back to her thoughts and me
to mine: the goose I saw
that afternoon while walking
out for the cattle, alone,
turned back north, no formation
to lead or follow, all the time
in the world in front of us.

Waving to a Neighbor Around Dusk

A snowplow scrapes the lot
below this window—metal drags
across asphalt and
the cackle and groan
of a three-quarter-ton truck
pushes the blade.
These sounds don't remind me of a farm.
I no longer wake at night
when I smell a breeze
carrying fumes of diesel or
top soil freshly turned under
and try to remember if I latched the gates
and shut the hog house doors.
The oak branch whacking its trunk
is not a barn door
flopping and slapping in the wind
but the man shoveling the sidewalk
across the street, a neighbor
I'll wave to when he looks up,
somehow resembles a Bud South
twenty years younger pushing snow
off his drive after chore time.
Once widowed, once divorced,
his daughter gone and his son
not yet yellow from cancer,
he's there beside a Victorian
surrounded by a windbreak
of eighty-year-old pine.
From the cattle lot I can see him
on his side of the gravel road
stretching south past other farms
with windbreaks and barns and north
into timber where it becomes sand
and impassable after rain, frozen
rough and drifted shut in winter.

We are surrounded by Midwestern space,
undulating hills and bare oak,
cottonwood and mulberry. Specks of cattle
spread across a pasture thirty acres east.
He looks up from his shoveling and waves.
I wave back.
We both return to the work in front of us.
Interstate 80 hums
five miles behind the yearlings
in the feed lot huddling against the wind.
There's a tractor hauling hay into a snow-packed field.
Tin lifts off the collapsed corncrib roof, shivers,
falls, hovers, clicks.
The mail is still in the mailbox
at the end of the lane. The wind
has stopped. Maybe someone will visit.

Thorn Tree

Sitting down to flip
through the pages
of a borrowed book
long past due, you
stumble on two
words—thorn tree—
their place on the page
and in the story touches
a spot you'd forgotten:
the timber rented
from a man called White,
owner of a tractor
with the same name,
its hard rubber lugs
dent the powder
soil lane leading
deep into the eighty
one acres of thick-with-
trees, too-steep-to-level
grazing ground, and
at the center a leaking
wooden water tank
guarded by a tree with spikes.
Then Mr. White
sits on his tractor,
blood dripping
from his cheek
into his torn work
shirt, onto the hot
metal platform between
the clutch and brakes, off
the grease-stained draw
bar, into the earth,
hard and baked.

On Elm Street

A young maple loses
its leaves before the season changes.
The sky remains
blue and the cornfields
are mute as I drive
to work, but I'm not sure if I
am driving or if I am sitting
still and the Iowa
landscape passes by. Maybe
it was yesterday, or
twenty years ago, the sun is coming
up and I am the fat kid
stopped for traffic on Welsh Street; the maple
leaves hold the growing light, then
drop it onto the chrome handlebars
between my hands. Maybe I am
thinking of the song on WMT I heard
while eating breakfast, or the dead
crickets blowing
in circles on the porch.
Say I was that fat kid,
I had a porch with dead crickets,
and a song in my head
while I waited for traffic, and
this morning I am in a car
on my way to work and I see
that boy waiting
for me to drive by so
he can peddle down North Street
to the edge of town.
It's pointless to tell him that distance
consumes the changing seasons
there and spits back silence;
it's pointless to tell him
twenty years will pass before he realizes

the maple leaf holds the secret
of light, and the dead return as
the sound of blowing crickets.

Imaginary Homecoming

This is where the cottonwood tree stood.
There used to be a dog chained to it.
The dog died first.

If you stand here you can see the barn.
You can see it from every point on these two hundred acres,
but this spot is the closest.

Here's a fence post—use your imagination—
that used to be a corner post
for all the fences on this farm.

Don't drink the water.
You used to walk barefoot across this
gravel drive just to feel the pain.

Those holes—you can see them
better at night—your brother installed
with his homemade throwing star.

Here you were run over by a tractor.
There you shot at a rabbit four times.
From the top of that bin,

the air feels better.
Here, I think this is what they told me,
you started to walk.

At Midnight Walking Home

Past the county jail,
the court house,
past the trees in the park
that remind me of willows,
but are more beautiful,
if there can be a tree
more beautiful than a willow
budged by the wind and
dancing with its shadow
across the street,
Market Street is deserted.
Red lights blink
then turn off First Avenue.
Alone again we have just walked
wordless to the library,
annoyed by the silence around us,
the space it creates between us.
I listened, but heard
only footsteps and breathing.
I tried to see behind the windows
above the square and
get my mind off the moment,
off my hands, but I
was confused and the trees
didn't help, and the empty streets
spreading east and west
added to the confusion
of whether I should be
back at the book drop
where we paused to say goodbye,
or here on High Avenue East
heading home. You pulled
my hand to your back
for one last embrace
then called me a fool

for letting you go.
Under the street lights,
aware of loss, aware of foolishness,
aware of the trees in the park I may never
know the name of, or in the darkness
surrounding me when I wake
with you on my lap, I decide
to take you home even though it's late,
even though I'm in love, even though
I'll never be finished with you.

Landscape with Leaves

If I say I love the leaves
it is the sound of leaves
scattering across brick
and moss, it is the concert
of crisp cackle and sizzle
I heard as a child
as I ran through them,
it is the susurrus murmuring
that feels like a woman's lips
brushing against my neck
by accident when she sleeps.
Standing here I realize
it has taken me twenty years
to discover this—
a walk along the river
with an apple and a thick sweater
and feet that have almost forgotten
the beautiful syntax of ground,
the language it speaks
through thickets of fallen
oak and elm branches and scatterings
of leaves made generic from the passage
of seasons—has been waiting
to mean I love the leaves.

Paseo de los Amantes

Any moment the phone might ring
and the neighbor will flush her toilet
then walk back to her kitchen,
her pots and cats. And
at a moment like this,
in Spain, Badajoz perhaps, the sun
is already sweating the street's
few remaining children tired.
All morning they have played with a ball,
which is really a flattened scrap of tin,
and they will wake from their naps and kick it
again before they go to bed for the night.
If they are aware of the couple
driving a black Opel Corsa
down Paseo de los Amantes,
music speaking to the heat
from the lowered windows,
they hide it well. They don't
complain about fatigue, no one
thinks of love. I could say
that everyone is tired and today
it might be true. I could say that
we are learning to bypass love
but that doesn't mean a thing
to the village children in Badajoz
who play with bent metal and want
to be men halfway around the world
carrying guns, holding beautiful women
or kicking a ball through a goalie's hands
as the last seconds tick off the clock.
Whoever said this world is about celebrating
what we do not have, and, if we hope
for a different life as we fall asleep
our wishes might come true, didn't know
his ass from his head.

I can only plan on lying in bed
dreaming I can play lead guitar
like the woman on the radio, speak
the language of the handsome
foreigner at the county fair, or be like
the man I saw twenty years ago
driving a '69 Austin, heading west,
heading away from where I stood.

Looking for Lorca Between South and North

I

I ask *Como se dice* and point to
the sky blue and clear beside the red sand
stone draped with vines falling from the Alhambra.

In the plaza we have beer
with everyone else
and a riverbed
filled with a sound
that isn't water.

Las Golondrinas
and she mimics
with her hand
the flight of a swallow
as it decides
then changes
its small mind
which part of the
sky it will fly.

In the language
of swallows its name
sounds like the Spanish
word for whisper,
feather, talon, and eye.
Its life is as long as
the number of wing beats
needed for flight
divided by the mass of what it fills.

You don't have to believe me.
Answers are only obstacles
made up of unjudged discoveries.

II

At the base of Amboto
in a northern village
Lorca never named,
a swallow
surveys the pasture.
There is a horse
no one rides, two
cows have just been milked,
twenty four million
shoots of pasture grass
are woven by the air
falling down the mountain.
The day only begins
as the fence posts splinter
through the fog-covered
meadows, the wires
stretching invisible, then
visible between them.
The sound of men slapping
wood with hammers
echoes across the valley.
The silence is vast enough
to hear a swallow memorize
the air beat under its wings.

Love Poem (Rewrite #507)

Without the awareness of the other,
without a nod of any metaphysical head
we one day die.

We reflect, become shadows,
fidget, think of the singular
past becoming plural present
and somehow a future singular.

We sit; you are no longer here
with me, but here in me, in
that chair's wooden seat,
in the chip-flecked cup.

We sat where I now sit:
present, singular, whole.

Landscape: Galicia with Two Figures

There is a church,
there are women
sitting in a circle
making gossip and lace.

The waves welcome then
turn us away.

There are always clacking hammers
in the distance, gulls and salt in the air
outside the bars
where we share *café con leché*
while boys play
a football match the future
of the world depends upon. Somewhere

in this I became the man who took
the hand of the woman you became,
a loaf of bread under his arm, in her hand
empanada wrapped perfectly by a woman
who left her shop to watch them walk away.

I'll Say it This Way

You are my 5th Avenue
You are my 6th my 8th my Broadway
You are my grain of salt my steak
      boiled baked and fried potatoes
      my sweet corn on the cob
You are my border crossing
You are my trans-Atlantic flight
      the long layover between London and Bilbao
You are my new pair of shoes
      the blisters they give my feet
      the sliced tomato in the fridge
      the smell in the sheets
      memory of your underwear drawer
      the cool in my drink
      humidity
You are the obituary on page A 17
      the sliver of photograph falling
      out of the folded-up letter I still
      haven't sent
You are radio static
You are the dream I had last night
      the night before
      I want tonight
You are the words
      I wish I'd written
You are anticipation
      the mistakes I've made
      the worst decisions I've made
      the moment I want to quit
You are the voice that says quit
You are the one for me
You two thousand miles away
You different languages spoken
You asleep right now while I write

Breakfast with the Neighbors

They're in bed.
They've forgotten
to lower their blinds
again and my breakfast
glows exhausted limbs and hair.
If only television
could offer such subtle
entertainment—a woman and a nude
man without a laugh track
falling out of love and forgetting
the words and tears that kept us
awake the night before, or
who they were
before they fell asleep, oblivious
actors for this man with toast
and a tepid cup of tea.
If they could see the sun
cast light across their thighs
as it does right now, her hair
covering his shoulders
like an out-of-place sheet,
her arm holding down
his chest woven into the bunched blanket
shadow of her legs, there
might be a way out of. . . what
is it called? The inevitable? Gold
and crimson bathed, they are in light
that makes me think I can see
their breath consuming the minutes
before they wake, or that I can
know what they dream.
I don't want to know.
I want what it takes
to be one person mingled with another
and content for the rest of my life.

I would settle for the leftovers
of morning, even be the glowing
lamp on the nightstand
beside them. I'd burn
my eyes across them.
I'd put myself out
when I finished.

The Cats of Fuchosa

The grocery in Apata is owned by a woman
whose son thinks he is a link in the chain
that will stop those causing the problems of the world,
so he has cemented his arms in the barrels
that cross the street to stop traffic, and he is waiting for the changes.

Outside the grocery where women watch
but don't care who comes or leaves
you can see the cats
behind the iron gate ending the street.

Today you are a woman beside a man
at the end of that street. Standing with her arms
across her chest, as if this familiar wind
blowing down Amboto touches or pulls at her heart
and happens to carry a sensation
and also a memory so concrete and irrefutable
she is aware of every breath, she
holds her elbows like a widowed mother.

Should she say what she sees
she would describe the cats as aristocratic.
Never mind the man.

And never mind the woman you have become.
Stand here and search for the right word,
put lineage in it if you want,
both the lineage of the cats of Fuchosa
and the memory of cats as you conjure them.

Don't forget the young man
stooping into a barrel of hardened concrete,
his arms linked like a chain, was a child
and like all children he will eventually pay
the high charge of treason,

though he will think he dies for a cause
called independence,
his comes from the day
he kicked a cat
as it became one of the cats of Fuchosa.

His mother will try to speak to him now
in the language of mothers,
but she has lost her fluency.

The man you ignored still stands
beside the fence looking in
where the cats used to linger.
He stays behind for the wind
to become familiar. He waits
for someone to be like the woman.

The Sound of Habitation

The woman I think I can love
is upstairs and
the man I want to be
waits in the basement
for the other woman
he desires to leave:

she is the silence
who sat beside him
in his car on
Hwy 92 east of Knoxville;
a frog leapt
from the foxtail to the asphalt
the moment a song became
popular, and he won't know
if it's dead until Tuesday.

Down here
the air is black, a spider
clings to its silk and
hangs a web on the basement
door. Each exists: one
is here drinking
from a glass that will fall and
shatter and make
the squirrels pause;
the other sips her coffee not
knowing Schopenhauer
said there is something
in us wiser than our heads:
that thing must be like
black spider silk,
the nut husk
a squirrel drops from an oak
branch, or that moment life

changes to death,
that instant ink
dries and coffee is cold
in the cup held like a hand.

III

Rush Hour in the City of Q

It is early morning or
late afternoon. Time's frozen
like a single frame of film.
Each face is different.
No two show the same emotion
or share the same glare.
One is thinking about his first night of love.
Another dreads her second day of work.
A mother looks for her son.
The man by the newsstand is looking for a wife.
A woman in furs watches her reflection in the store window.
Behind her, the old man looks toward the sky with closed eyes.
A businessman considers a crime.
The one with the umbrella doesn't know he is about to be fired.
The woman in the taxi thinks about her shoes.
The man stepping off the curb thinks about the rains he heard
       talked about on the bus.
The one leaving the bank contemplates leaving his wife, children,
       this life.
The man in front of the woman thinking about the money in her
       husband's account is about to faint.
The cyclist is about to sideswipe the taxi; the taxi is running a red light.
A blind woman stands in the middle of the sidewalk, touching an
       empty space in front of her.

Landscape with Swallows
I

I am in Iowa, on the edge of town
and all the space in the world
will never help. Or the sunlight.
Or the omelets I make for my wife
so she can remember
La Gran Via and Las Ramblas.

She wants to be a bird
flying above Barcelona
until she tires.
She wants to sit on someone's sill
and watch the streets
as if from their eyes.

She hardly sleeps.
She moves her hands in circles above her head.

Her baths are long.

The bed and her shoes
are too big. Each night she tells me
I might wake and find feathers on our sheets.

II

She has grown fearful of sunrise.
It melts the frost on the foxtail,
discolors the sky,
the power plant steam. She says

the squirrels in the oak
have started to treat her like a bird;
they are aloof; she is offended.

III

Life would never be as it had been
when the birds with silver-blue bellies
flitted and glided from chimneys to trees.

They played with shadows
all afternoon like a child surrounded by space,
grass and time. A day to sit

and watch swallows fly: forgotten or never
known, beauty flying,
shimmers above the ground, radiant.

IV

She wore a feather
hat. Her favorite
color, a rush
of black, red and blue—
just like moments
before sunset.
She thinks her soul
is filled with the beauty
of what remains
after it has gone, after
the sun has set, and dark,
like the tail tips
of swallows,
covers us.

V

Now she wears her favorite gown—blue,
sleek echoes of dark, the back open
as if leaving room for wings.

Her feet have become invisible.
She no longer listens when I say
I don't have feathers on my sleeve.
The air around her
becomes sacred when she sleeps.
Her eyes are always moving,
her lungs beat urgently.
The shower water glides off her skin.
She has become small
enough to fit in my hand. She fears
she hears noises unlike other noises.

VI

She stands on the corner
of Elm and Birch,
skin shimmering
in front of the sun,
watching the maples,
the traffic thin,
the sound of tree-hidden swallows.
She picks at the threads
clinging to her sleeves.

The sun sets.

The trees are silenced.
Feathers the color of sky
fall from the branches,
black tipped as if singed
by fire, as if mimicking
the approach of night.

VII

Every morning I descend
the steps so I can
be here waiting for the sun to rise.
At this moment
I'd like
to be shoes,
the stretch
of gravel roads,
the dark, a plank gate
slap against the barn,
the smell of leather,
of cattle, dung covered
hay and straw,
a speck of grain dust.
The sky burns as if
lit by shivering swallows,
the tips of their tails.

In High Demand

I led a blind man astray this morning,
took him to the middle of an open field
then drove away.
I took candy from a child
then pushed him into a puddle.
I took change from a fat panhandler
then told the police to arrest her for loitering.

Tomorrow I'll give a stranger the wrong directions
and won't leave a tip after lunch.
I'll misguide your children
and lie to the priest.
If there is anything else to do
you can count on me.
These are troubled times.

Landscape in the City of Q

for Idoia Elola

Today someone's stock plummeted.
Yesterday a forsythia petal
shuddered and the day before
the homely boy next door whacked
the Jones' mum to death.
From the west a gust,
the north a gale, the south
and east quiet as the sky
sweeps down on another sobbing neighbor.
Enough of this silence
can make noise: a filled
library, spinning alarm clock
sprocket, that bend in the road
where cars have stopped to look
at the view, the words on a page
pawed by wind. A photograph
propped on a desk—a woman
standing on a bridge motioning
with her finger—gathers dust,
bends in the sun.

I Can't Do Anything Now

I'm awake with a pain in my chest
that feels like the knife stuck
in me as my boy
asked for some money
and I know I need to change.
It's time to get to work.
I've got a weekend
and no wife,
not enough money for trouble
so I can sit in the yard and read,
I can pick the rotting concords
from the vine and suck the juice
and spit out the skin until my thirst is gone.
If I think of the pages I told myself I should read
everyday and how many I've read since then,
subtract those from the others,
I've got my work cut out for me.
Just like I should paint those window frames,
strip the porch swing so I can sit there
if the rain what's-his-name said was coming comes.

But then there's you.
You've trapped my heart
and peeled back my spine.
I can't eat, sleep or drink now
without thinking first
of you, that fall
of hair dividing your shoulders
or splashing your face. I see a spot
under the tree I think is an oak
and it has shade;
it's close to the house and big
enough to keep the neighbors guessing.

I have to go. This always happens.

I've got my work. I get started
and you come along. You cut
into me, push and pull,
these thoughts of you,
something has to change.

At a Friend's House in the City of Q

After Hikmet

The corners hung with cobwebs.
The ceiling first, I guess
and then the corners. . .

We sit with our
elbows touching, our feet
under the sheets touching.

The stove clicks in the corner—
it's not enough to warm the room;
we have flannel sheets and two quilts—
and there is snow drifting against the window,
sifting through the screen, climbing the glass.

We're reading and I don't need to ask if you're happy.

Give me your hand—always smaller than mine,
no matter how it surprises me—and
put down your book; your face
shows the sleep that waits in the corners.

I still love the color of your eyes—
your pleading soul—your
lips on my neck, your hair over
your shoulder.

The heat is unbearable—
I am the cause;
the window is open,
the sheet pulled down
exposing my legs, here
in another country, in bed
in the dark, thinking of where
I went wrong and why

I'll never know,
I write ignorant
of where you might be.

After the Procession of the Virgin of Solitude

Imprisoned in her winters,
in her nights, her folds
of endless gown and under
her bolder-thrown gaze,
her thorn-tree embrace,
they learn to love and give up.

His back cracks and her ears burn
at the sound of swallows
tearing at their bath.
The sky and afternoon
wilt like the lilacs
left on the river bank
beside their empty clothes.

Afterlife

When I return as an ant
or quarter inch of head lice,
I'll have learned

that mountain beyond I wanted
to climb is even bigger now.
I'll know the width and length
of a horseshoe just in case.

I'll remember how the Egyptians
made paper, and I tried too,
but kept swallowing the celery
before I could chew it to a pulp.

On the Outskirts of the City of Q

There are days
when city sounds
do not reach these
vacant fields.
If they do,
they resemble those
badly dubbed films
one sees rarely these days—
the white and yellow
earthmover belches
smoke and proceeds
down the trash
heap, in its cough and
clatter the man
replacing shingles
does so without volume,
and then, as if remembering,
releases the *thwack thwack*
which ricochets off
the utility poles.

Out here, no trees,
only weeds and up-turned
dirt, rubble and smoking
squatters' huts with boiling pots,
children's chatter, a raised voice,
but most often music drifts
in opposing directions.
There's a useless plastic
fire truck cracked in half
the children have found
a use for. A dog's about
to die. No one knows
what this place was.

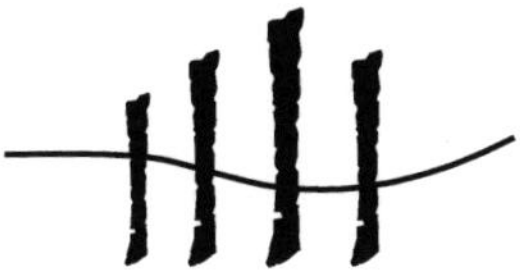

During a Lull in the Conversation

He said it rained slabs of ice
somewhere in north
Texas, in the panhandle,
and held out his hand to show
just how thick and wide.

We were crammed into a corner—
three of us—around a table
with tea and cake,
imagining geometries
falling from sky.

The three of us were silent
after that, each looking out
at a different New England,
at the few flakes of afternoon
beginning to fall.

A Birthday Present that Resembles a Poem

The light behind the immense oaks
lining this path looks like snow falling.
Outside the park it is midnight
the 9th of July and I once had a brother
whose birthday—today—
makes him a thirty-year-old man
I no longer know. If I called,
his wife would answer. She wouldn't
recognize this voice
or name and she'd ask
for a message and repeat
happy birthday
as if the words carried solemnity.
I'd apologize, or tell her
about my life: *I have plans,*
my luck has changed.
Maybe not. Instead,
I could describe the sky: *it is back-lit,*
as if someone were shining
an uncovered bulb behind the trees.
I'd explain that waiting
for the moment when it burns
out isn't as bad as it seems.
I'd say, *It's beautiful. I didn't think*
it could snow in July.

Waiting

Birch leaves push the breeze and spring
has loosened another stone in the wall.
The oleander has started to bloom.
No grass grows on this path. The stable
has fallen into itself and with it the sounds
it once held: rope stretched
between cow and gate, hoof thump
against flesh, ears flapping away flies.
Spring smelled and sounded like this
when I was a child.
Any minute a crowd
will walk through this gate.
By now they should have passed
the vineyards, but they do not arrive
and my mind pushes them further away.
The squirrel crossing the path
with a bread crust—or is it a twig?
I can't tell from this distance—
might be dead and decomposed
where his feet just buried a walnut.
This wall, without cleft, will need new color by then,
but perhaps some child considers this now
as ants climb between his toes.

Action needs forethought just as war needs death.
It's a thought. Better yet, war, like poets,
should not exist. Why do I think this
when next year the hair clipped from my head
will remain scattered somewhere beside the stone
where it was cut? My enemies will again find me
and attempt to prove me wrong. The sky
blue or black, the moon full or crescent,
these words recalled or forgotten . . .

I'll try to keep my foot from the puddle.
I'll share the salt; we've all got wounds
that must be purged. I'll share my fire;
we all need a good branding now and then.
I'll remember that I know more because
I know that I know nothing.

Here they come. Where have you been boys?
Give me your ears. Today we learn to die.

Landscape with Crows

The crows are heading south
this afternoon. There is always one
as I climb College Street and
cross through the park where
the drunks read in the gazebo or sit
watching and waving to the new
mothers pushing their children
on the swings, laughing like the ten
crows climbing up through the maples
and oaks as I pass Dodge and veer
toward Burlington and Highway 6,
their critiques trickling down over the sorority
houses and three story houses broken
into crowds of student rooms.
Now there must be fifty darkening
the approaching evening
above what I've always called
bean stalk trees, but are really
catalpas as I turn down the alley
where Levis lived when he was here,
where I like to think
he wrote about linnets and the grape
cutters, because here there are no
linnets or grapes, or burnt hills
beyond which spreads the endless Pacific
and time confused with depth and blue.

We repeated an hour
twelve days ago,
as if we were back in grade school
and had sinned—
spoken out of turn, thrown an eraser,
or pencil, or said *fuck* and meant it—
and now we have to sit
waiting in our corner as the afternoon

drifts out of reach, our
punishment the early dark
pulled over us by the crows
drifting south, and our corner is
a state in the middle of a country on
the edge of winter.

I've tried to count them
but these birds
have become the dark
surrounding this window.
My neighbors have come and gone,
the balcony shaking and the stairs
wobbling under their weight.
All I can do is envy
every day at this hour, fear, never
know where they are
coming from or going.
Maybe the fields lining the Cedar
River, or circling Solon
or Cedar Rapids and now
they are flying down
through West Liberty where the rent is
cheaper, where the Hispanics have
taken over Main Street and the first
string positions on the football team.
Maybe they are completing that enormous
circle Stern talked about, one so big I
can only see a straight line. Maybe
they are lost. Maybe they've given up
and tomorrow they won't be back.

Blue

Do not look for ink, a wild iris, book
jacket or fish, but the space between
button holes on a worn shirt,

the waitress, her fingers touching
your fingers, her veins,
her dress, your eyes, the plate.

Think of the words you recited, their order
on that crisp morning they rose
like flame burning dry leaves; they waited

like breath hanging in front of your closed mouth
the morning of the first frost, the morning
your boots shattered the grass, you breathed

a cloud that lingered, expanded, faded.
Think of it as a kettle's voice. Think of it
as the window crack sealed with tape.

Inside

No one here to hear
my falsetto sing this
morning rereading
what I read last night
looking across the quad
at the ground, at
the trees outside
a drapeless window,
a woman's hand
climbing a man's back,
his mouth moving as if
telling me . . . what
I should expect
from the silence
between two.

I need gloves,
I said for him,
soon it will be cold.

A Sound Like Footsteps Beside the Ocean

for Vincent Cioffi

Someone—I will say he is a boy
on his way to school because it is
Wednesday and the blinds
are closed—walks through the leaves while
I realize I am content
to sit at a desk,
on a second hand chair and
watch the sunrise as the coffee
brews and the traffic sits at
the intersections waiting for
that moment the light changes.

The trees are bare and I know
if I had roses I'd pick them
before they froze, that I am not
thirsty but I want coffee, that, because
the sun is up and the coffee smells,
there must be someone like me
two thousand miles west: a man who thinks
he is watching the light enter
his room and gather on a wall in
the form of a girl he once loved;
her voice like water
pulling sand over sand.
He tries to hear the waves
to see if she still
loves him but the mechanics are
turning trash cans into exhaust
pipes. It is morning,
the last month of summer. Beneath
his window a cable flops against another cable,
a boy kneels to tie
his shoe, a rose scowls

at the top of a teetering stem. The leaves
wait; they gather in
impatient groups and wait.
The sun fades his wall
like it fades this one, his eyes, like these,
close slightly as they consider sleep,
the wind taunting the leaves
into sounds like footsteps.

Afternoon

Basil makes me feel like summer,
makes me think of dinner,
sex, a beer afterwards in bed. . . .

I wash my hands and the walls are still white,
the potted plants dying, the TV and stereo still waiting.

Last night, a woman's voice
pleaded with me on my phone
for all the time I could spare.

She sounded like the one who wanted me
then didn't. She laughed when her jokes weren't funny.

I told her to be patient, that I try
to be concerned with the affairs of others
but mostly I'm alone, and I stand in the dark
talking to myself. Her pause was long,
understanding I think, before she hung up.

Sketch

The angler
stands beside a stream,
the dew that covered the grass stems
dried under the light
falling from a sun
hanging under a monochromatic sky.

Along the shore a tree bends
and touches its shade.
He has removed his hat and
a breeze has frozen
his thin hair onto a brow
pale like the belly of a catfish.

Today is no exception—
his basket will rub
against his shirt and tackle
as he walks along the path inclining
to a house set apart from others.

His wife and child,
now laughing
and playing with dolls
in the kitchen, will fall silent and
recall their distaste for fish
at the sound of his heavy boots.

Portrait of an Evening

I will be reading tonight
when a car pulls off the road,
bucks and clicks through foxtail
and milkweed and parks half in
and half out of the Skunk River.
And tomorrow, when no one
finds the broken body, the crushed
sternum behind the wheel, the dust
will still be floating in the sunlight
above this armchair.
This window without a view,
that woman across the street
on her bed attempting to master loss,
are oblivious to what lingers
in the shadows behind the road
signs warning of S curves.
But right now when
a car crosses Highway 63
and raises dust that ripples back
into the night like a wave
in a sea I don't know exists,
when the tires cling to the gravel
on the second curve of a road
without a name, all this remains:
somewhere a man will have
a list of things he needs; a place waits
for a body to fill it; a woman sits unnoticed
by her husband. Somewhere
a clock stops when it is five o'clock.
It is five o'clock somewhere and
here it is not. A child disappears
when he closes his eyes, and the sideways
glance of a beautiful woman falls on a letter.
Somewhere the dead are only dead.

A Reason for Concern

I'm not sorry that today is
the beginning of fall. I'm
not sorry I can't
see what floats above New Jersey
or the George Washington Bridge.
Nor that I sat for eleven hundred
miles so I could be here
watching black birds
graze among acorn husks
on my back lawn. The squirrels
wake me and keep me
awake at night. Days
have turned into years,
and I'm not sure I can be pushed and filled
and remain the way the wind moves
the maple leaves, the way the branches
accumulate chattering
black birds, the way these oak trunks
refuse to splinter outside
my windows. I don't believe
the woman I sleep with
when she tells me I talk in my sleep.
I don't believe in the language that makes
me want to fall in love
with sounds, in the black birds
telling me I won't understand, in the squirrels
ignoring me walk down the street.

A Splinter Becoming a Burning Plank

If you run your hand down
the length of a 2" x 6" piece of age-smoothed pine
to feel the grain of the wood and you
don't lift it in time to keep the timber
from becoming part of your palm,
like you became part of the girl
everyone had kissed by the end of summer
in a ditch beside a gravel road,
the pain you feel isn't immediate
like the sky above you or the ground
humming between your feet. So
you might look at the four-inch splinter
piercing the flesh that used to be yours
and consider a word like *acumen*, or *sapience*;
you might think of the farmer who fell
from the hay loft onto a pitchfork
upturned in the manger
then walked to the house
to die in the arms of his wife,
but now the pain is rushing
your mouth and can't wait to squeeze
out, reckless like suffering built
up over time, and you wonder
if words like *love* and *death* have
anything to do with a splinter, with
a cracked piece of pine useless like
an image that has been folded too thin
over years to hold a memory of desire or duty
from wandering through
like the steers standing on the lawn
the morning the farmer walked out
of his house to feed them.

They stood as if the feedlot
had a welcome mat

and they'd wanted to wipe
their hooves before stepping back
into the rain-cleansed lot, but chance
left them dumb with new freedom
to track the green lawn a black
that would take months
of rain and heat to erase.
They were out because they could be,
because the posts and planks
that stretched to make a lot
had shattered in the herd's silent push
out of the barn, and
before they were aware of place
they stood outside the lot looking
in at the others looking out,

like the night twenty years before
when you sat in a ditch with a girl
and two other boys and waited your turn
for a kiss. The men at the party stood
at a cattle tank filled with beer and ice
and smoked and talked while the women
whispered at the picnic tables. Someone
shouted above the music, above the yellow
yard light creating a line of hidden and seen,
for more rocky mountain oysters,
more beer. Laughter rolled across
the lawn like soft wind through summer
tall weeds, and the cattle nudging through
the dark in the pasture beside the ditch and
the corn across the road standing
in its communal murmur watched it pass.

Each boy was having his turn.
Young enough to feel your heart

leap with each kiss, you were the inexperienced
son of a farmer who would one day hire
you out to her father. Was she responsible
for teaching you more than desire or
was her kindness the agonizing death
waiting on the tines of a pitchfork? If you say
she held your hand while she kissed your
brother and that changed your life forever,

say you have thought about that kiss
every night, and didn't know how to
remember it so maybe none of this
would have happened. Now
there should be silence and open space,
and dark because it's almost winter
and you have not seen any of these things.
You are in this poem because I don't have
the courage to say I've forgotten
it was me touching the lips of a girl
in the dark, feeling the stab of a splinter,
or that the man falling on the pitch fork
was really my grandfather who fell through
the floor of a corncrib and walked to his
house on a crushed ankle but didn't
want to die or be held by
the arms of the woman he didn't love.

Ninety-seven was the worst year, and I am back
at the barn where I watched my hand
become foreign. The wind stopped blowing
three months ago, after the night
it mowed the windbreak pine and dappled
the barn and house roof with holes.

The fallen trees are piled below

the cottonwood waiting for someone
to start the fire that will burn the sun-dried
leaves and pine needles, the twigs and branches
caked with sap that will catch and pull the flame
inside and bellow smoke out to lose itself in
the color of bleached sky.
This man sits while I stand; we watch
the fire grow and the air fill with ash
as old as the wind that carries it. The empty
sound of the barn and corncribs, the cattle lots
and farrowing house are disguised as wood
snapping and fighting the fire's heat, unwilling
to burn before its time—there is no use.
Like the splinter inside my palm,
like this man fallen through the floor, like
the boy after he'd acted like a man, the fire
catches and burns from the center out and
fills the air with sparks that catch the hog house
roof and a pile of planks this man remembers
lay in its rafters. Maybe he knew their worth
and mine, maybe he asked if I would save
the wood because he'd lived his life saving,
maybe there was disgust and despair
in his voice when he'd realized
I hadn't learned what he wanted.

If the wood was a man waiting to die,
and the flames licking the rafters a man
waiting to forget, nothing would change.
I refused. Fear is easy in the face of fire,
beneath the shingles trickling tar drops,
under the weakened rafters collapsing
and the planks popping and snapping
inside the shrinking walls, but salvation
is a trick to make us think.

We watched, my grandfather squinting
from his chair, me standing with my hands
in tact, wondering if anything turned out
the way it was planned. If I could say
the wrong fire was started by the wind
that splintered the trees, and the wrong boy kissed
the wrong girl, and the wrong man was dying
in the chair beside me I would pray
to the god of smoke and the god of stench
and the god of this man's thoughts
to become the wind and blow this fire
down to a lingering flicker that won't burn
the charred bark to cinders and scatter it
across the fields, but leave the fire-hollowed
trunks broken and black, oblivious
to the rain and wind and let them both
creep slowly back into the ground.

Curtis Bauer's poems have appeared in Barrow Street, The Asheville Poetry Review, The American Poetry Review, and numerous other journals. He is the publisher of Q Ave Press Chapbooks and teaches Creative Writing and Translation at Texas Tech University. Fence Line is his first book.

For information about the John Ciardi Prize for Poetry, contact BkMk Press. The prize has been awarded previously to Steve Gehrke for *The Resurrection Machine*, selected by Miller Williams; to Tim Skeen for *Kentucky Swami*, selected by Michael Burns; and to Terry Blackhawk for *Escape Artist*, selected by Molly Peacock.